D1394555

Easyway Guides
Brighton BN2 4EG

© Straightforward Publishing 2010

British Cataloguing in Publication data. A catalogue record is available for
this book from the British Library.

ISBN 9781847161635

Printed in the United Kingdom by GN Digital Press Essex

Contents

Introduction

Introduction

Now, more than ever, in the middle of the worst recession since the 1930's individuals need to understand the workings of the stock market. The economy has been ravaged and shares in many major companies have plummeted, in particular the banks. The would-be investor has been put off in a major way from investing as the economy goes into a tailspin.

Experienced investors have lost their shirts and if they have, what about the inexperienced investor. What should he or she do?

This book is intended for anyone who wishes to understand more about the workings of the stock market and also the whole culture and environment of shares and share dealings.

It is true to say that until recently the ownership of stocks and shares and the workings of the stock exchange were a mystery to most people. Shares and the stock exchange were seen to be a specialist areas dominated by the well heeled and, invariably, the public school boy, the old-tie network.

Times have changed and now share ownership is within everyone's grasp. This has been so because of changes in the ownership of former public utilities and the dispersing of shares to the ordinary person. Alongside that has come an opening up of the whole area of share dealing.

By discussing the nature of investments, the operations of companies, the stock market, the nature and costs of shares and also the interpretation of data in financial pages, this brief introduction to the stock market should provide enough information for the smaller investor to operate with confidence and to make informed decisions.

By investing carefully, taking time to analyse markets and regularly reading financial data, the small investor can prosper on the stock market.

****

1. The Individual Investor

The investor

Individual investors can be defined as people who, after meeting all their expenses from their income have a surplus left which they wish to invest, one way or another. There are many reasons for investing, the main one being to meet future needs. Investors can keep a cash reserve in a building society or bank, they can invest in something that they think will appreciate in value, such as property, or shares which can be resold when needed.

Purchasing assets

Assets come in many shapes and forms, cash, premium bonds, securities such as shares in a company or gilt-edged stocks (which are government issued bonds), life assurance policies, works of art, property and so on. Each type of asset has different characteristics which will appeal to different investors. The subject of this book is the stock market and therefore we will be discussing stocks and shares as a viable investment.

The first characteristic of an investment that needs to be considered is an annual return: does ownership of a particular commodity entitle the investor to receive any income and if that is the case, what is the level of that income?

Income can be realised in a number of ways. There is the good old fashioned deposit in a bank or building society, which will give a monthly quarterly or annual return but not at rates that will excite the adventurous investor. Gilt-edged bonds pay interest each year, again guaranteed but relatively low. Investment property will produce a rental income and will appreciate in value (in the good times) and the purchase of shares should, in the ideal world, produce a dividend and possibly capital growth, depending on the share. Again, like everything, the more solid investment, as we shall see, such as in companies characterised as 'Blue Chip' companies, will generally produce stable but lower returns.

An investor will usually consider the return on an asset as an annual percentage of its value. This is the rate of return, or the yield. The rate of return on a share is known as the dividend yield and is calculated in a similar way to interest from a bank or building society: the dividend paid by a company is divided by the price of the share as quoted on the stock market. Dividend payments on shares are not guaranteed. Companies, for a variety of reasons, can decide not to pay a dividend. However, the other rate of return on shares, capital appreciation, is an equally important consideration to an investor.

Capital appreciation is the increase in value of any money invested. If inflation is higher than the rate of return then money will lose value. Shares are similar to other investments in this respect. They can fall in price as well as rise. Essentially, the total return on any asset comprises income received and the increase in value of that asset (capital growth).

Investors will need to look at the possibility of loss on assets. Different assets have different degrees of risk, usually relating to their potential for appreciation or depreciation. Deposits in banks will rarely if ever depreciate as periodic interest will be added and the investment will be protected apart from a possible loss of value due to inflation.

Ordinary shares carry risks of both falling prices and falling returns. A company's declining profits can result in a fall in the share price and also lead to a company deciding not to pay dividends. Many investors will usually try to create a portfolio of shares, ranging from more high-risk equities to safer homes, so that a fall in the value of one is offset by the growth in value of another.

Basically, different assets have different degrees of return. The main principle is that the higher the return the higher the risk.

Investors will also take into account the degree of ease with which they can convert their asset into cash if need arises. This is known as the liquidity of an asset. The liquidity of an asset will affect the return received. The more liquid an asset, as a general principle, the lower the return. Asset liquidity and asset values are also affected by time. For example, the longer that money is tied up in a bank account the more illiquid that it is. Because of uncertainty about the future, money today is worth more than money tomorrow. To bring their values into balance, and to encourage saving and investing rather than spending, the longer that money is unavailable in the present, the greater the reward.

Hedging and speculation

When weighing up which assets to buy or to hold, an investor will keep coming back to the main consideration: risk. The more risk-averse investor will want as much protection of their assets value as possible. There are various means of achieving this. One basic strategy is called hedging, and it is a version of the strategy of portfolio diversification: the investor will hold two or more assets whose risk/return characteristics to some degree offset each other. One typical example is to hold one safe but low return asset for one high-risk one. A more precise way to hedge is to use derivatives, the range of securities whose price depends on or derives from the price of an underlying security. We will be discussing derivatives later in the book. A put-option, for example, gives its owner the right, but not the obligation, to sell a share at a fixed price (the striking price) on or at a certain date. Owning a put option with the share itself means that the investor's potential capital loss is limited to the loss implied should the share fall to the striking price. If it falls further the investor can use the option and sell at the striking price.

The speculator

On the other side of the hedgers trading is the speculator. This is someone who is prepared to take on the extra risk that the hedger wants to avoid. Speculators are in the market with the intention of making as much money as possible. They believe that they know the future prospects for asset prices better than the majority of investors, and hence are prepared to take bigger risks.

Investors, whether hedgers or speculators, who expect a rise in a particular asset price or in the market as a whole are known as bulls, whilst those who express pessimism about the future of the markets are known as bears.

Markets

Assets are bought and sold in markets. Markets are institutions that allow buyers and sellers to trade assets with one another through the discovery of prices with which both are satisfied. Some traders may meet in physical places. However, in the age of technology this is not necessary. Wherever and however the trading is carried out, what is actually happening is a form of auction. For example a trader may have 100 lots of assets to sell If there are more or less traders at the suggested price (more or less than 100) the trader will lower or raise the price accordingly. This becomes the current market price.

Financial markets can be classified in different ways. One basic distinction is between primary and secondary markets. In primary markets, new money flows from lenders to borrowers as companies and governments seek new funds. In secondary markets investors buy and sell existing assets among themselves. The existence of the secondary market is generally considered to be essential for a good primary market. The more liquid the secondary market, the easier it should be to raise capital in the primary market by persuading investors to take on new assets. The secondary market allows them to sell should they decide that it is an asset that they don't want to hold.

Markets may also be classified by whether or not they are organised, whether they are regulated by an institution. For example, the London Stock Exchange is an organised market while the over-the-counter derivatives market is not.

Markets can be classified by the nature of the assets traded on them: stocks, bonds, derivatives, currencies, commodities and so on. All of these are distinct markets and there are strong connections between them. These connections grow stronger as increasing globalisation and improved technology allows better flows of information. An investor will need this diverse but interlinked information to allow them to compare and contrast different investments.

2. The Company

Companies

Companies are organisations established for some kind of commerce and with a legal identity separate from their owners. The owners are the shareholders who have the right to part of a company's profit, and who usually have limited liability. This means that their liability is limited to the value of the shares that they own.

Companies are often run by people other than the owners, although in theory it is the ordinary shareholders who control the company. However, the ordinary shareholders will be the last in the queue of claimants should a company go under.

Companies can be classified as limited liability or public limited companies. It is with the latter that we will be concerned here as PLC's as they are known are listed on the stock exchange and their shares are traded on the market, such as the UK Stock Market.

Company data

The primary source for any data and for analysis of a company is its annual report and accounts. These documents will provide all the information on a company's business and financial affairs and its obligations to its shareholders. We will be looking at interpretation of company accounts later in the book.

The annual report and accounts will describe the current trading conditions of the company, what it has sold (its turnover, sales and revenues) and what it has paid out in wages or salaries, rent, raw materials and any other inputs to the costs of production.

The documents will also indicate the profit or loss position, the state of assets and liabilities at the start and end of the financial year and the cash flow situation.

Profit and loss

A company's profit and loss account is a statement of the final outcome of all its transactions, all revenues and costs during a given period, usually a year. It shows whether the company made any money in the previous year, how it made the money and how it spends the profits. Comparisons will also be made with previous years and also with other company's performance.

The total value of all goods sold by the company is known as its sales or turnover. Deducting from the turnover the costs of producing goods will give you an operating profit figure. Deducting from that figure, in turn, the costs of interest payments to banks and other parties, will give you a pre-tax profit. It is this profit that is reported in the financial pages.

The next deduction is tax. Corporation tax is paid by the company on profits after all costs have been met except for dividends paid out to ordinary shareholders. Advance corporation tax, which is income tax paid on behalf of ordinary shareholders and their dividend income, is also payable. Money left once taxation demands have been met is known as after-tax profit or equity earnings. This is now at the disposal of the company for distribution as dividends or reinvestment in the business.

The balance sheet

The balance sheet is a snapshot of a company's capital position at an instant in time and details everything it owns (assets) against everything it owes (liabilities) at year-end. The two sides of a balance sheet, by definition, should balance. Essentially, liabilities are monies borrowed to invest in assets.

A companies assets are made up of two items: fixed or long-term assets, such as building and equipment; current and short term assets, such as stocks of goods for sale, debtors or accounts receivable and cash in the bank. Its liabilities are made up of three items, the first being current or short term liabilities, such as trade credit or accounts payable, tax, dividends and overdrafts at the bank and longer term debt such as loans and mortgages etc.

The third form of liability is that of ordinary funds and this in turn divides into three forms: revenue reserves or retained earnings-the company's trading profits that have not been distributed as dividends; capital reserves-surpluses from sources other than normal trading such as revaluation of fixed assets or gains due to advantageous currency fluctuations; and issued ordinary shares.

Ordinary shares have three different values; their nominal value, the face, or par, value at which they were issued and their book value which is the total of ordinary funds divided by the number of shares in issue; and their market value, the price quoted on the stock exchange.

Cash flow statements

The cash flow statement details the amount of money that flows in and out of a company in a given period of time. The cash flow statement will track flows of money.

The balance sheet is a check of a company's financial health, and the profit and loss account is an indicator of its current success or failure. Together they can be used to calculate a number of valuable ratios. We will be looking at company accounts later.

Companies raising finance

From the perspective of a company, the financial markets exist to raise money through various financial instruments. There are basically three sources of capital: permanent capital of shareholders (also known as equity capital, ordinary shares or in the USA, common stock); ploughed back profits (equity funds or shareholders reserves): various forms of debt or loan capital.

Corporate finance will usually focus on the relative benefits of financing via debt or equity. The relationship between debt and equity is known as gearing (or leverage in the USA), which we will look at later. The more highly geared a company is the more its borrowings compared to its share capital or turnover. A highly geared company will suffer more from interest rate changes and so on. The ratio is calculated as follows:

Total debt liabilities = long-term debt + current or short term liabilities

Balance sheet gearing or
Debt equity ratio (per cent)
$$\frac{\text{Total debt liabilities} \times 100}{\text{Ordinary funds}}$$

Income gearing is an important ratio. This indicates a company's ability to service its debt.

Equity

Equity finance is the capital that allows companies to take the risks inherent in embarking on new business projects. This equity finance is derived from shareholders. There are two common classes of equity capital: ordinary shares, which have no guaranteed amount of dividend payment, but which carry voting rights; and preference shares which usually carry a fixed dividend and have preference over ordinary shareholders if the company is wound-up but carry no voting rights. There are basic variations on these which are discussed throughout the book.

Companies listed on the stock exchange and wishing to raise new equity capital would normally do so by a pre-emption rights issue. This means that existing shareholders have first option on the new shares or the right to sell that option. An increase in the number of ordinary shares in a company without a corresponding increase in its assets or profitability results in a decrease in the value of the shares. This is known as dilution of equity.

To avoid immediate dilution of the shares in issue, a company might use an alternative financial instrument to raise capital, a convertible (also known as a convertible loan stock or a convertible bond). These are debt instruments that can be converted into ordinary or preference shares at a fixed date and price in the future. Their value to a company, besides avoiding dilution, is that in exchange for their potential conversion value, they will carry a lower rate of interest than standard debt.

Company debt

An alternative to share capital as a source of finance is loan capital. This kind of finance is attractive to companies in that it allows the business to be developed without relinquishing ownership and is often more available than equity capital.

Like equity capital, corporate debt takes several different forms. Long-term loans are normally raised by issuing securities; the most common form in the UK is the debenture. Most debentures offer a rate of interest payable ahead of dividends and are often secured on company assets. They usually trade on the stock exchange, involve less risk than equities, but pay a lower rate of interest than other debt.

Other forms of loans include fixed and floating rate note, and deep discount and zero coupon bonds. One of the most recent innovations in debt instruments is the junk bond, a form of finance developed in the USA. This is a bond that offers a higher rate of interest because of the risk entailed. In the 1980's junk bonds were used for the takeover of large companies by relatively smaller ones. They marked an infamous decade with some 'junk bond kings' being imprisoned.

3. The Stock Market

The Stock Market

Having looked at the general operations of companies which trade on the stock market, we can now turn to the actual stock market itself.

What is a stock market?

Most people know a market as a number of stalls, trading outdoors, from which you can buy almost any commodity. You can buy fruit and vegetables, clothing, travel goods and so on at an outdoor market. There will be the usual smattering of Del boys and Arthur Daly's. A stock market has the same features, buyers and sellers, an agreed price. However in stock markets you will usually also have a middleman, essential to guide the investor through the maze of dealings on offer.

There are many recordings of the first known stock markets in European Cities. In Britain, the first recorded joint stock company was founded in 1553 to finance an expedition to the orient, via a northeast passage. Two of the ships sheltered from storms in Scandinavia and all the crew froze to death. The third reached Archangel and then went overland to Moscow-which was as near to the Orient as they got, and agreed a trading link with The Czar Ivan the Terrible.

There have been many similar ventures. Alongside these ventures London's financial institutions grew. The London Stock Exchange grew out of a small coffee house-the New Jonathans Coffee rooms. As the business grew they moved and eventually in 1801 acquired the name the London Stock Exchange. There used to be a number of stock exchanges dotted around the country but they were eventually amalgamated into one exchange in Old Broad Street London, next to the Bank of England. The stock exchange has since moved as it has had to increase its space as time has moved on and technology and the world markets have grown more complex.

There are two elements to the London Stock Exchange, the first being the official list, which is the main market of the major companies. This is further divided up into groupings by trade. There is a section for distribution, banks, breweries plus one for Techmark (or techMark as it is known) for high-tech companies. In addition there is the Alternative Investment Market (AIM) (see below) which is for young companies that do not have the trading record demanded for a full listing.

Stock markets now are remote from companies and deal electronically. London's main market operates on a computerised system called the Stock Exchange Electronic Trading System (SETS) for large shares, with a modified version for mid-market companies. SETS is an order matching system that pairs off the instructions sent to the machine by buyers and sellers. At the moment the smaller shares are using a system called SEAQ, which is based on an American system. The completed deal is passed to another computer to organize settlement. The Crest system is trying to eliminate the mass of paper by replacing share certificates with an electronic record. Share certificates are still available for those who want them.

Other UK markets-The Alternative Investment Market (AIM)

AIM is usually known by its initials and is a division of the stock market reserved for small businesses. The idea is that the smaller business will grow and mature and graduate to a full listing. The costs of listing on AIM are almost as high as a full listing. However, the hurdles for acceptance on the AIM are lower. There are about 750 companies from a variety of countries listed and the number is growing.

For the smaller investor in Britain there is an added attraction in that Aim listed companies are regarded by the Inland Revenue as unquoted, thus providing access to differing tax relief schemes, including business taper and gift relief for capital gains tax, suitability for the Enterprise Investment Scheme, relief for losses and business property relief for inheritance tax (see section on tax further on in the book).

The downside, and there always is one, is that smaller companies are less secure and more vulnerable to financial problems

TechMark

The London Stock Exchange launched techMark to deal with the business of high tech businesses, given their importance to the future. The principal aim of this sector is to attract companies involved with new technical ideas - including the Internet – with the promise of rapid growth in their field. As we have seen from recent history, the dot-com boom and bust, this is a risky area for investment and needs a degree of knowledge and also faith in the future of the various ventures.

Ofex

Ofex is one of the growing number of competitors to the main London stock market. Ofex is a derivation of off-exchange. The

Ofex system was started in 1995 and trade is done on a computer owned by a stock broking company called J Jenkins. It is a matched-bargain system, so the deal only goes through if there is another willing buyer or seller feeding an order into the computer with a similar view on prices. The fees are fairly low for this type of system.

Virt X

This incorporates a small rival to the London Stock Exchange called Tradepoint, which started as an electronic order book in 1995 and was itself quoted on AIM. In combination with the Swiss Stock Exchange SWX, it created Virt X, with offices in London and Zurich. In addition to trading in the normal UK quoted stocks, it has set up clearance and registry systems to allow trading in Eurotop, the 300 largest companies in Europe.

4. Shares

Shares

Before discussing further the workings of the stock market, it is necessary to have a clear idea of what a 'share' is. When businesses start up, whether large or small, they need money to commence business, expand and then grow. For many businesses, indeed the majority, the initial seed money will come from savings, loans, re-mortgages, friends and family. However, at a later stage of development a company might need to obtain capital from other sources.

Shareholders

A Shareholder is either a person or an institution who, in return for an investment, will purchase shares in a company. The origins of share purchase go back several centuries. A shareholder is not a lender of money but is an owner of the business, or part owner. This means, essentially, that the managers of a company are employed by the shareholders. The shareholders have the right to appoint, and to fire, the board of directors and will, at the end of each year, expect a dividend on their shares, as interest on their investment. Whether or not a dividend is paid depends on the performance of the company.

The stock exchange

In the usual run of events, a company that issues shares will be a 'public company' and will be listed on the stock exchange, which regulates the way that public limited companies do business. The origins of the term 'stock exchange' goes way back into history with no one really knowing where the term came from although there are numerous theories. Essentially, shares mean part ownership of a company which is the simplest way of understanding the term.

Once a company gets quoted on the stock exchange, there is a continuously updated price for the shares which, usually (hopefully) is far higher than the original share price. There is also a steady stream of people who are willing to buy shares in the company so once an investor puts the shares on the market it is likely that a quick sale can occur, unless the company has obvious problems.

Blue chip shares

Shares have differing status. Obviously, despite reassurances to the contrary, shares can go down as well as up, and investing in the stock market therefore is a gamble. Many people have lost their proverbial shirt 'playing the market'. It is for this reason that lots of investors will turn to the safest companies, those long established companies with a track record of success. These are known as 'Blue Chip' companies. Take a look at the FTSE Index of Shares (the 100 highest performing companies, all blue chip) and you will see that the high performing companies are usually the older companies, such as ICI or the petroleum companies. They have financial muscle, can invest and absorb risk and hire the best managers. The downside of investing in such companies is that the returns are on the lower side, but are stable. The gamble is reduced but returns lower.

Blue chips, like all shares, can never be totally safe. If you look at companies which were on the list a few decades ago many are no longer in existence. So, the gamble, slim though it is, is still there.

Tracker funds

Tracker funds buy most of the shares across the FTSE 100 index so that they avoid being prey to the problems of just a few. In other words, they spread the risk and ensure a steady flow of dividends.

Shareholder benefits

As mentioned, a shareholder will get a dividend on his or her investment. This is a return on the share value. If the company has done well then the value of the share will have increased too so when it is time to sell then there will be an increase in value on their original investment. Shareholders are also protected in the event of a company going bankrupt in that they can only lose the value of their shares and no more.

It is true to say that longer term shares have proved to be a good investment, trumped only by property which, until the current recession and severe house price downturn, had shown spectacular increases over the last 10 years, with investors receiving a return by way of rental income and also through capital appreciation. Sadly, this is not now the case, although rental returns still constitute a good investment.

Types of borrowings

Businesses issue a variety of 'paper' which are used to raise capital. In addition to raising capital from shareholders, a company may need to borrow in the short term and longer term and may issue bonds or other forms of paper.

For borrowings a company may issue what is in effect a corporate I.O.U. This will come in the form of a bond. Bonds can be traded, are long term with an undertaking to pay regular interest, at a rate fixed at time of issue (normally) and with a specified date at which they must be redeemed. Some of these bonds are backed by assets of the company and some are unsecured. Like all loans, the interest rate will reflect the status of the bond.

Loan stocks and debentures

Bonds that have no security are called loan stocks or notes. Debentures are underwritten by assets. These types of paper are different from shares in that, notwithstanding the performance of the company they must be repaid at the specified time. Shares, as we have seen, do not.

As the rate of interest on bonds and debentures is fixed the market price of the paper will go up as interest rates go down and vice-versa. This factor underpins the attractiveness or otherwise of bonds as an investment. Because the rate is fixed at issue the investor knows how much the return will be, assuming the company stays solvent, right up to the date of redemption. Any investor in bonds will need to look at the company as a whole and its future prospects of staying afloat before investing.

If an issuer defaults on repayments, usually because of going bankrupt, debenture holders can appoint their own receiver to realise the assets which act as their security and repay them the capital. Unsecured loan stockholders do not have this option but will still rank ahead of shareholders in repayment. There are different types of debentures which will take preference over each other depending on the nature of the paper, i.e. subordinated debentures will have less preference than an un-subordinated debenture.

Warrants

Warrants give the owner the right to buy ordinary shares (equities) usually over a specified period at a predetermined rate, which is known as the strike, or exercise, price. Warrants have a definable value and are traded on the stock market, with the price directly related to the underlying shares. The value is the then market value of the share minus the strike price. For example, if the share currently stands at £2 and the cost of converting the warrant into ordinary shares has been set at £1.50 then the price of the warrant would be 50p. If the shares then increase to £5 then the price of the warrant would be £3.

Preference shares

Preference shares give holders similar rights over a company's shares as ordinary shares. However, usually, holders do not have rights to vote at company meetings. Like bonds they get specified payments at fixed future dates. The name, preference share, signifies their privileged status, since holders of preference shares are entitled to a dividend whether the company is making a profit or not. This obviously will make them attractive to investors who want a fixed income. If the company is not in a position to pay a dividend on a preference share with cumulative entitlements, then the dividend will be 'rolled up' and paid in full when the company is able. Preference shareholders rank higher than ordinary shareholders when it comes to dividends. They rank behind debenture holders and creditors for liquidations and dividends.

There are combinations of various classes of preference shares which will be set out when the shares are purchased.

Convertibles

Certain types of preference shares and corporate bonds are convertible. This basically means that during their lives the holders receive a regular dividend income but there is also a fixed date when the issues can be transformed into ordinary shares. This conversion is at the owner's choice, not the issuers.

Gilts

Gilt is short for gilt-edged securities. These bonds are held to be safe and dependable. They are issued by the British government and, by virtue of being backed by the country as an asset, the risk is seen as zero.

Gilts are issued because politicians mortgage the future of the country. For example, when tax revenues are suffering, because of a dip in the economy, government bonds will be issued. They have a fixed rate of interest and are redeemable at a specified time in the future. There are normally a range of specified dates to ensure more flexibility for the government. The interest rate at issue is determine by the prevailing interest rate and also the target audience, who the specific issue is aimed at. Most gilts on issue are of this type.

There are index-linked gilts and also irredeemable bonds, such as the notorious War Loan, issued to people who backed the national effort during World War Two. Unfortunately, people who backed the war effort ended up with virtually nothing as inflation after the war eroded their value.

The list of gilts being traded along with dates of redemption is extensive. There are shorts (lives of under 5 years), medium dated (between 5-15 years) and longs with over 15 years to redemption. Most quality newspapers carry lists of these bonds and rates of interest.

These papers will have the 'yield' rate, one being called the running yield, which is the return you would get at that quoted price and the redemption yield which calculates the stream of interest payments and also the value of holding them to redemption and getting them repaid-always at £100 par, the face value of the security. Since the return on the bonds is fixed at issue, when the price of gilts goes up the yield goes down. Therefore, if you buy a gilt with nominal face value of 100p (£1) and with an interest rate set at issue of 10%, but the current price of that issue is 120p, you would get a yield of 8.3% (10p as a percentage of 120p). If the price of that issue falls to 80p you could get a yield of 12.5% (10p as a percentage of 80p).

There are, in addition to gilts, other public bonds issued by the government at a slightly higher risk. These include bonds issued by local authorities in a bid to raise money, and also overseas governments. The risk is very slight indeed. It is not likely that a local authority would renege on its bonds. Obviously, if you invest in a bond in a country which then undergoes revolution of one sort or another you may be holding worthless paper. It is up to the individual to assess the risk.

There is a very marginal rise in the interest rate of these bonds, because of the perceived slightly higher risk.

Derivatives

Derivatives markets will trade in various things that depend on or derive from, an underlying security inherent in that 'thing'. This security will determine the price of the investment. Basically, there are financial products derived from other financial products. The term 'derivative' is usually taken to cover futures, options and swaps. There are many other complex instruments, some of which are detailed below.

Futures
Futures contracts in the financial markets are generally used by companies and investors in order to protect themselves. The risk will be 'hedged' or offloaded. For example, a business exporting to another country can shield itself against currency fluctuations by buying 'forward' currency. That provides the right to have a currency at a specific rate at a specific date, so that any income from overseas sales can be more accurately predicted.

A futures contract will bind two sides to the agreement to a later transaction, whatever it might be. It is a specific obligation set out to buy or sell an agreed investment or product at an agreed date. For example, an investor decides to buy a futures contract of £10,000 (whatever it might be for). It costs only 10% margin, in this case £1000. Six months later the price has increased to £15,000, so the investor can sell at a £5,000 profit. The opposite can be true with any investment, the price can go down as well as up.

Futures contracts can be sold before the maturity date and the price of the contract will depend on the price of the underlying security.

There is also something called an 'index future' which is an outright bet, similar to backing a horse or other bet, with the money being won or lost depending on the level of index at the time the bet matures. An extension of this is 'spread betting' which most people have heard of but do not understand. The spread betting company. for example will quote a company's shares at 175-200p If you think that the shares will rise by more than that you 'buy' at 175p in units of £10. If you are right and the price goes up to 210p the shares have appreciated by 10p and you have made a profit on your investment. However, if the share price falls then you have made a loss. If the price remains within the same price range then no one wins. Only a small amount of money is paid at the time the contract is made, so the potential profit margin is geared up. This is helped by the absence of capital gains on the proceeds, because it is a bet. This activity, spread betting, is a fast growing activity. However, as with all betting, many people have lost a lot of money and warnings have been issued by the Financial Ombudsman and Financial Services Authority. My own advice would be don't touch spread betting if you have a limited knowledge of the financial markets and of share movements.

Forward contracts
As we have seen, a futures contract is an agreement, about commodities, currencies and financial instruments. Two sides to the contract agree to do a deal at some time in the future. A forward contract is a deal there and then, but for a future delivery. The contract is at a 'spot' price (the price currently

prevailing) with a specified date for completion when the goods arrive.

Options

Options provide the right to buy or sell something as opposed to obligations contained within a futures contract. Someone for example, might option film rights for a future date. In relation to shares, buying a 'put' option, as it is known conveys the right to sell a set parcel of shares (usually 1,000) at a specified price at an agreed time. Because the price has been fixed at that time if the share price has fallen then the investor can make a profit. And, once again, vice versa. The opposite of a 'put' option is a 'call' option where the investor has the right to buy shares at a fixed price in the future. A profit is made if the shares rise substantially in the interim period. If they fall, a loss is made. All that has been lost is the margin of option money.

Options can be traded before maturity. This is known as 'hedging' ones position. For example, if someone knows that they will need funds in a few months time, to fund an acquisition, then if there is a worry that the market may fall in those months, then this is a way of buying protection: buying a put option at roughly today's price.

A basic example is if a company's shares are standing at 65p, it could cost, for example 6p to establish the right to buy shares at that price over the next three months. If the shares go up to 95p in that time then the investor can buy and sell immediately and make a profit of 24p. Like all our other examples there is a downside. If the shares fail to rise above 65p then a loss of 6p has been made.

The situation works the other way as well. If there is a suspicion that a company is about to lose serious value then someone can buy a put option-the right to sell the shares at a specified price-within an agreed set of dates. These rights have a value as well, related to how the share is performing and how long they have to run, so they can be traded, mostly on the London International Futures and Options Exchange (Liffe).

Covered warrants

Covered warrants are fairly recent. They are a more flexible option which is easy to deal with. They originated in Germany in 1989 and are very popular indeed. A covered warrant is the right to sell or buy an asset at a fixed price called the exercise price up to a specified date called the expiry date. This expiry date is anything from three months to five years at issue. The warrant can be based on a whole host of financial instruments or commodities. As with other derivatives investors can use covered warrants to gear up their speculation, as a way of hedging against a market change or for tax planning. Covered warrants are issued by banks or other financial institutions as a pure trading instrument. Covered warrants can be American (exercised at any time before expiry) or European (exercised only on specified date). If a warrant is held to expiry then it is automatically bought back for cash with the issuer paying the difference between the exercise price and the price of the underlying security.

A covered warrant costs less than the underlying security: this provides an element of gearing so when the price of the underlying security moves, the price of the warrant moves further. Warrants are a riskier purchase than the underlying security. A relatively small outlay can produce a large exposure and that makes warrants volatile. They can produce a large return or lose the complete cost of the warrant price, called the premium.

Overseas shares

As with major U.K companies quoted on the stock exchange in London, there are a number of large European and other companies listed. Most of them trade in the U.K so it is possible to get a clear idea of the business patterns and also to invest in them.

The merger of European stock markets has made it relatively easier to gain access to overseas shares. There are a large number of internet based stockbrokers in Germany, France and Holland which make the task easier. You can buy overseas shares through a U.K. based stockbroker, however only a few offer such a service.

If you intend to purchase shares in overseas companies then it is very wise, as with all other share purchases, to carry out some research. There are added levels of risk with overseas shares in that information concerning important variables such as interest rate movements and the economy as a whole, plus the state of particular sectors may not be readily available whereas information concerning the U.K economy is and the overall level of knowledge is greater.

In addition to the above, there is the exchange rate risk. Profits from share trading overseas may be affected by movements in exchange rates.

Shares and investments/unit trusts

There are benefits connected to the purchase of unit trusts and investment trusts as opposed to individual shares. With trusts you get a spread of investments over a number of companies, cutting the danger of one of the companies going out of business.

Investment trusts

Investment trusts are companies which invest in other companies on behalf of investors. They are termed close-end funds because the number of shares on issue is fixed and does not fluctuate no matter how popular the fund may be. This sort of investment is convenient for small investors who do not have enough money to buy a lot of shares in different companies thereby spreading the risk. An investment trust will have its money spread across a lot of companies so problems with one company will usually be compensated by a boom in another company. Managers of investment trusts are professionals, so, at least in theory, they will do better than the average person. It is true to say that investment companies are as good as their managers so it is wise to pick a company with a good and known track record.

Most investment funds have a lot of money to invest and they will usually invest in blue chip shares, unless specifically set up to invest in a specific type of share.

The cost of the stockbroker is the same as it would be with other dealings and the government stamp duty and the price spread between buying and selling price remains the same.

Although investment trust managers do have a lot of say in the nature and type of investments, investors will also have some say in what goes on by buying the right investment trust shares. There are trusts specializing in the higher risk stock markets such as Budapest, Istanbul and Madrid (called emerging markets); there are some investing in the Pacific Rim and some concentrating in Japan; some go for small companies and some specialize in Europe and the United States and so on. The spread of investments can be very diverse indeed and managers of investment trusts tend to be more adventurous on the whole than managers of unit trusts.

Some trusts are split capital trusts which have a finite life during which one class of share gets all the income, and when it is wound up the other class of share gets the proceeds from selling off the holdings.

Trusts are quoted on the Stock Exchange so the share price can be tracked and also the asset value of the trust can be calculated. The asset value is comprised of the value of the shares that the trust is holding compared with the trusts own share price.

One main reason that many are priced differently than their real value is that major investing institutions avoid trusts. Huge pension funds or insurance companies do not have to buy in to investment expertise as they normally have their own experts. Therefore trusts are used mainly by private investors.

Unit trusts

Unit trusts have the same advantage of spreading risk over a large number of companies and of having the portfolio of shares managed by professionals. However, instead of the units being quoted on the stock market as investment trusts are, investors deal directly with the management company. Therefore the paper issued has no secondary market. The investor cannot sell to anyone other than back to the management company. The market is seen from the manager's viewpoint: it sells units at the offer price and buys them back at the lower 'bid' price, to give it a profit from the spread as well as the management charge. Many unit trust prices are published in quality papers.

These are called 'open-ended' funds, because they are the pooled resources of all investors. If more people want to get into a unit trust it will issue more paper to accommodate them. Unlike the price of investment trust shares, which is set by market demand and can get totally out of line with the market value the price of units is set strictly by the value of shares the trust owns.

Tracker funds

Tracker funds move with the main stock market index, in the U.K that is usually taken to be the FTSE 100. This type of fund is for the less adventurous investor who looks for a virtually risk free return.

Open-ended investment companies

Open Ended Investment companies or OEICs are placed midway between investment trusts and unit trusts. They are incorporated companies and issue shares, like investment companies. Like unit trusts the number of shares on issue depends on how much money investors want to put into the fund. When money is taken out and shares sold back, those shares are cancelled. The companies usually contain a number of shares segmented by specialism. This enables investors to pick the area they prefer and to switch from one fund to another with a minimum of administration and cost.

Advantages of pooled investments

Pooled investments reduce risk and are therefore a safer home for small investors. However, as they are safe they are unlikely to hit the outside chance of a high performer, as individual share speculators might.

As stated earlier, there are many different companies and a certain degree of research and knowledge is essential before committing. To be forewarned is to be forearmed. Quality newspapers will have regular league tables of performance. Be careful too with tables that are published showing performance. Obviously, tables can only look backwards to demonstrate past performance and it is the future that matters. Trusts can do very well, but it may be that they have done well in a sector that has expanded and is now contracting.

Management charges for both investment trusts and unit trusts are usually high. One way of avoiding high charges is to opt for a U.S. mutual fund, which is the same as a unit trust and which has lower charges.

There is also the alternative of setting up your own investment vehicle which has become quite popular over the years. Investment clubs, already very popular in the United States are springing up in the U.K. Basically, a group of people together pool cash for investment in the stock market. The usual way is for each member to set aside a regular amount each month and decide where to invest it. This has the advantages of avoiding charges, spreading investments and also the social spin off. Also, the work of researching shares is spread amongst members.

Exchange traded funds

Exchange traded funds are single shares and are traded in the same way but are in effect representative of the whole index, such as the FTSE 100 or the U.S Standard and Poors 500. It is like an investment trust with a holding in every company comprising one of the indices, but there is an unlimited number of shares and the price is directly related to the index. There is a slight deviation from the underlying portfolio price but it is very narrow. That also means they can be used in the same way, including 'selling short' and included in the ISA's. For a small investor it has the comforts of a unit or investment trust plus the reassurance of not outperforming the market. That means you will never do better than an index but will never lose all your money. There is no stamp duty on the dealing because they are Irish registered companies although there is a small management fee charged by the issuers, usually 0.5%.

5. Owning Stocks and Shares

Owning shares

When looking at shares as opposed to other savings and investments, it has to be said that the number of ways a person can invest amounts of their hard earned cash is limited.

There are a whole range of savings accounts paying varying rates of interest, ranging from mediocre to relatively high (at the time of writing the base rate is 0.5%), all dependant on what you want for the future of your savings, i.e. instant access, long term growth and so on.

Property has proved to be a good investment over the years, particularly with the advent of buy-to-let mortgages. An investor could realise an income and also growth in capital value. As mentioned this is no longer the case and many people who took out these types of mortgage are now in trouble.

Moreover, this type of investment is not for everyone, particularly because of the high capital investment at the outset.

Art is another area of investment but again not suitable for everyone as it requires specialist knowledge when purchasing in order to ensure capital growth.

There are a whole range of other collectibles which rely on at least a basic level of knowledge at the outset. Wine is one area and antiques another.

Because most people need access to their capital to fund a whole range of short and longer term projects, such as holidays, education and so on, buying shares usually ranks way down the list as an investment.

Shares are usually a longer-term investment and the risk involved in the investment depends on the timescale of that investment. Rewards can be measured more easily if a longer term has been allowed to elapse.

The stock market provides a fairly good home for investments for those people who are prepared to accept a degree of risk and can wait for the right moment before cashing in and pulling out. Essentially, money invested in the stock market should not be money that you need to realize at short notice or money that will be realized for your old age. The stock market is only for people who have spare cash to invest and can weather the storm if a loss is made. It is not for those who will lay awake at night worrying about losing money on shares. True to say, the last few years have turned dreams into nightmares.

If you do decide to invest in the stock market, and there are about 12 million people who have done so in the U.K. then don't put everything you have to invest in the market at once. Keep some aside to invest when a really good opportunity arises.

There are two ways to invest in the stock market, long term (suitable for the small investor) and as an active trader.

Long-term investment

It is true to say that in the long term the stock market has produced a better return on investment than any other alternative form of investment. All of the charts produced to indicate growth have demonstrated that over a period of 30, 50 and more years, returns from shares outperform most other investments. Shares in Britain have, since 1918, produced a return of over 12% a year compared with other investments such as government issued gilt edged securities which have produced just over 6%.

This return on shares has been in the face of the periodic cyclical downturns in the economy and in overseas economies. Cash in a deposit account would have produced 5% in the same period. However, cash in a deposit account is safe and as we have seen shares can be a risk.

When considering the long term, questions of future economic stability will always arise. For sure, at different periods economies will fluctuate (the current recession being the worst since the 1930's) and losses will occur but in the longer term these tend to even out and share prices rise, as history has demonstrated.

It is up to the investor to decide what they want from an investment. Do you want income or capital growth? These are not absolute alternatives, since companies that do well hand out handsome dividends (usually) and see their share price rise. Unit trusts and investment trusts as we have seen provide good homes for savings and, at the very least will ensure inflationary growth.

Short-term investments

This is another way of investing, but it is for the experts and people who are sufficiently clued up and will devote time to study the markets. This is the short-term active trading which is built on the tactic of taking advantage whenever share prices move sharply enough to make trading beneficial. The active short-term trader will watch the markets very carefully and look for opportunities such as takeovers and mergers where they can buy and sell relatively quickly at a profit. Short-term investing usually requires more money than longer term investing as the costs of trading can be higher as brokers fees and government taxes have to be paid.

Perks of owning shares

In addition to the usual benefits of owning shares, such as appreciation of capital and dividend income, many companies try to keep shareholders loyal by offering perks, usually in the form of discounts of one form or another. Channel tunnel has travel concessions offered to shareholders, other nationally known companies such as Iceland and Kwik Fit all provide benefits to investors. A number of fund managers will provide a list of companies that provide perks for shareholders.

6. Costs of investing

Costs of investing

When considering the initial amount to invest in a parcel of shares, it is important to realise that the less you invest the higher the overall cost of shares, because of fees etc and the more a share has to rise to make a decent return. It is for this reason that most people in an advisory capacity would say that £2,000 is the minimum that should be invested.

For safety the investment should be spread over a number of companies. The old adage 'don't put all of your eggs in one basket' rings very true here. A common portfolio for a small investor should contain at least 12 companies. The main aim of all investing is to get a decent return with the minimum acceptable risk. If you own shares in one company then the risk and possibility of losing your money is greater than if the risk is spread.

It is a general rule that the lower the risk the lower the return. However, the converse holds true, the higher the risk the higher the return. For some people who invest in a single company the rewards can be big if the company does well. In truth what usually happens is that large investments in one company will not produce massive returns or result in loss of all ones investment. The shares will usually carry on rising marginally in the longer term.

Investment clubs

We discussed investment clubs earlier in the book. We saw that they are an alternative to funds managed by professionals and as a result can keep costs down. Investment clubs are a group of private investors who pool their money and decide collectively how it should be invested. There are now over 7,000 investment clubs in the U.K.

The ideal number of people in an investment club is usually between 4-20. If the membership exceeds 20 then HMRC will term the club a corporation and corporation tax will be payable. There are several stockbrokers, including major banks who have ready-made packages for investment clubs, such as Barclays and Nat West.

There is a specialist charity called pro-share which publishes a handbook on how to start an investment club. The advice contained in this handbook is very useful indeed because, although it is not absolutely necessary to have an in-depth knowledge of the stock market when joining an investment club it is at least useful to know something about the different sectors that you will be investing in.

For investors clubs there are model rules and constitutions that need to be adopted. As with all collective endeavours, from residents associations to enthusiasts clubs, rules and guidelines are essential. Investment club rules will set out, for example, how members can join and leave the club, a unit valuation system that is to be adopted, the decision making process, levels of monthly subscription, meetings, appointment of officers and so on. It is of the utmost importance that procedures are followed as disaster will almost certainly ensue.

It is important to look at whether the club will run indefinitely, accumulating a portfolio or whether it has a specific life, say 5 years.

An investor might be invited to join an existing club so it is important that these rules are already in place and that they are the right ones for you.

A few other tips. Only join in with people that you like and trust. Ensure that their objectives and goals are the same as yours or it could end in tears later down the line. The criteria for choosing investments varies widely from club to club but many will go for the riskier end of the market because the club membership is additional to a members own personal investments. Some investment clubs will go beyond the stock market and invest in property either directly or indirectly through another vehicle.

The main advice given to any club member or would-be member is not to invest in anything that you do not understand. Avoid the overly complex and riskier markets such as derivatives, unless you have an expert on board.

Most clubs invest a small sum, it could be under £80 per month, so this type of investing is just as much fun, and social, as it is serious money making. There are some investment clubs who have had runaway success but, on the whole it is for the smaller investor with other aims in mind.

The cost of dealing in shares

Share dealing can be expensive, particularly in Britain. It is the case that it is more expensive here than in many other countries, and also the whole process is more complex, at least for individual shareholders. True, there have been moves by high street banks and other companies to make the process more transparent but it is still the case that small shareholders find the process rather confusing. It is also the case that small shareholders are still perceived to be a nuisance, because they deal in small amounts of money which cost just as much to transact as larger deals.

Commission

Commission paid to stockbrokers constitutes the main cost of dealing in shares. Commissions vary depending on the nature of the work and the type of broker. Rates of commission can vary anything from £5 per transaction up to £20 with commission on a sliding scale above the minimum depending on the value of the transaction. An order of £2,000 might cost 1.5% with the rate falling the higher the transaction. There can also be a one-off charge of at least £10 for joining Crest, the UK stock exchanges registry of share holdings.

There are several internet sites, such as www.fool.co.uk which provide information about brokers commissions. It is worth looking at this site before going ahead.

The spread

As well as brokers commission there is the cost of trading. Shares are like other commodities, the costs of buying and selling shares will differ. This difference is known as the 'spread'. Spread varies with risk. Big companies listed on the FTSE 100, such as Barclays, British Airways etc have huge market capitalisations and many shareholders with regular deals every day so would have a narrow spread of say 1-1.5%. A company with few shareholders and little trade would have a spread of up to 10%. The result is that for shareholders of small companies the shares have to rise even higher to realise a profit. There is lots of free advice concerning shares. However, it is true to say that for the small, first time investor even free advice can be confusing and misleading, given that this advice is often slanted in favour of whoever gives it. It is therefore advisable to use a stockbroker who is seasoned and knows the markets well.

For those with a larger share portfolio it is possible to sub-contract out the management. The stockbroker managing the portfolio will advise on investments but leave the final decision to the investor. The value of portfolios has to be high however, and this will not usually be the route for small investors. In addition to portfolio management there is discretionary management where a fee is paid to an advisor to provide advice on shares and also the timing of share purchase. The fee paid is quite high, or is based on a percentage and is therefore only useful for those with bigger portfolios.

Income tax

Another consideration to take into account, after everyone has taken their cut, is that of the ever-present HMRC. The government will take its cut by imposing a tax called stamp duty at the rate of .5% on the value of every deal that has used taxed income. The French and German governments do not impose such a tax therefore money can be saved by investing through these exchanges.

Buying shares

The process of buying shares has become markedly easier over the last few decades. In fact, many people have acquired shares through privatisations and through building societies becoming banks, and have not had to use a stockbroker. However, if people want to buy shares in the usual way there are several routes.

The first one is finding a stockbroker. Years ago, this was out of the reach of the small investor. Most stockbrokers operated within exclusive circles. Many did not want to be bothered with the small investor who knew very little, if anything about the markets. Banks have entered the arena with share dealing services and so has a new breed of transaction only brokers (who buy and sell but do not offer advice). However, more and more information is becoming available, through the internet and in newspapers. There has been a trend to present information in a plain English way and the information regarding shares is no different. Finding a broker over the internet is probably the easiest way to get started.

The internet has undermined the closed nature of share dealing and there are a large number of independent companies, most of which are members of The Association Of Private Client Investment Managers and Stockbrokers (see useful addresses). Many have their own web sites.

There are two types of broker: those who give advice and management (if appropriate) and firms who trade only. Phone based and online brokers are of the latter type.

People who think that they need help and advice can go to one of the big high street financial institutions with branches round the country. They can also seek out a good local firm that is experienced in the needs of small investors. The best way to find such a firm is by recommendation (like a lot of things) or you can go to the Association of Private Client Investment Managers and Stockbrokers.

As mentioned earlier there is the choice of advisory or discretionary services on offer. The latter, discretionary service, is for the larger investor with over £50,000 in their portfolio (although this figure is not fixed and can be lower).

Before picking a broker, ask questions such as how easily contactable are they and other terms and conditions.

7. Using the Internet

Internet broking

Internet broking has, like many other activities on the internet, grown massively. The internet has a lot of real advantages. Investors can place an order whenever they feel ready and can do it from any place any time. In addition, an enormous amount of information is available online to assist with decision making.

Dealing on the internet can also be cheaper. It is possible to deal over the net for a flat fee of £10. This is important for those who plan to be active investors and to whom the fees paid are crucial to profit margins. One Paris based research outfit called Blue Sky reckons that the four best value online brokers are all German. Although some online brokers require residence in that country before they will trade, Belgian, Swiss and Luxembourg brokers will trade with anyone regardless of residence.

One acknowledged problem with the web is that it is hard to get a picture of the reliability of the firm that you are dealing with. The web is largely faceless so there are risks of various sorts, such as hacking into your data and so on. Online trading does not generate a share certificate. The shares are registered to the new owner but it is still computerised and the broker will hold the title to them in a nominee account. This can mean that the investor cannot easily change allegiance to another broker.

To join an online stockbroker, you need to get on to a website and follow instructions for registering. Almost all will require cash deposited with the brokerage. Interest is paid on this money at a low rate. When signing on you register a password which provides secure access for the investor.

If you want to invest in the US you might want to go through a US based broker. These brokers are cheaper than European counterparts.

There is a site that compares the overall performance of several online brokers, this is:
www.europeaninvestor.com

There are two sorts of dealing online: one is to e-mail an instruction to a broker who will execute it via his trading screen. In theory he can do that within 15 seconds and within 15 minutes the deal can be confirmed. The other method is called real time dealing in which the investor connects directly to the stock market dealing system.

Normally, when the instruction is given, the broker will 'transact at best'-buy at the lowest available price and sell at the highest. The broker can be set a limit-the maximum at which you are prepared to buy or the minimum price below which you are not prepared to sell. Usually, such limits last for 24 hours although can be longer.

Once the transaction is complete the broker sends a contract note detailing the deal and how much money is to change hands. It may take some time to receive the share certificate but the important element is the presence on the share register.

8. Costs of shares

Finding out costs of shares

The London Stock Exchange has nearly 3,000 companies quoted. There is also the Alternative Investment market (AIM), TechMARK, and Ofex. Most quoted companies are traded infrequently with the most movement taking place within FTSE 100 companies. The FTSE 100 is the main indicator of trends in the stock market. Its name derives from the Financial Times Stock Exchange 100, devised between the FT paper and the actuarial professions. The major companies within the FTSE represent a significant proportion of Britain's industry and exports. There is a large concentration of institutional investment in those companies. The FTSE will change at times to reflect values of companies, which go up and down at times and will always have the top 100 by value. The moment a company drops out of the index its shares will take a fall.

Below the top level in the FTSE 100 there is another tier made up of the next 250 companies measured by market capitalization. Market capitalization means the aggregate value of the issued shares.

All of the above 350 companies are in the lists of the broadsheet papers price pages, which usually contain other companies as well. However, the list cannot be comprehensive such is the volume of the information.

Newspapers will also display a range of other information, including movements in share prices from the close of the previous day. Prices of shares in big companies move continuously and newspapers are often out of kilter with the actual price at any one time. To compound the problem the price printed is the mid-market price, that is the average of the buying and selling price. The internet is one place where accurate up to date information can be found, sometimes for nothing as at www.investment-gateway.com

The spread

Anyone who has bought a second hand car or holiday money will know that the price at which you buy is higher than the price at which you sell. Shares are the same. The difference between buying and selling-termed 'the spread'- will depend on a range of factors that affect the dealer's risk. One is termed liquidity: how many shares there are available and how many people there are prepared to trade in them. A good measure, as far as the stock market is concerned is how much the price moves when you trade. Massive companies have millions of shares on issue and there is always someone wanting to deal with them. By contrast a small company with a relatively small market capitalization and few shares being traded is difficult to deal with. Therefore, it is easier to buy and sell shares in the bigger companies than in smaller companies. The spread is wider in small, harder-to-trade companies. The width of the spread also depends on the state of the market. In wildly fluctuating shares, market-makers are loath to stick their necks out and carefully widen the spread.

9. Interpreting Financial Information

Interpreting the markets
-reading the papers

It is very important to be able to interpret the range of information that is printed in newspapers each day. The frequency and extent of the information will differ slightly depending on the newspaper. In this chapter we will concentrate on the UK equities market as this is the area which most small investors will be interested in.

As we have seen, an equity is another word for a share or stake in a company. The owner of the share will, hopefully, receive a dividend annually and will enjoy capital appreciation. The equity markets in the UK trade shares across a wide range of companies, from established and stable blue chip companies to the more high-risk ventures.

Although many newspapers do provide information concerning the equities market, and the information is the same, in this chapter we will concentrate on the best known paper dealing with financial information, the financial times, or FT.

The financial times gives in depth daily coverage of the equities market and this consists of the following elements:

- A report daily of the most interesting trading features of the stock market.
- The share price of individual companies.
- Various financial ratios
- Reports on individual companies

- Stock market indices indicating overall progress of equity share prices.

The London share service

The London share service is just about the most comprehensive record of UK market statistics available to the general public and covers around 3,000 shares. The LSS is divided into different industrial classifications. The share service covers companies listed both on the main stock market and also the Alternative Investment market (AIM), discussed earlier.

The standard version of the share service is published in the FT from Tuesday to Saturday in the companies and markets section. The table below indicates the way the information is presented.

Aerospace and defence

| 1 | 2 | 3 | 4 52 week 5 | | 6 | 7 |
| 8 | | | | | | |

Notes	Price	Change	High	Low	Yield	P/E	Vol 000's
BAE Systems	229	-2.5	291.5	199.25	3.3	16.8	35.419
Chenning	490.5	-1	491.5	373.5	1.9	13.4	79
Cobham	1367	-32	1460	1237	2.3	14.5	370
Hampson	21.75	-1.5	30	18.25	- 78.5	.5	262
Meggitt	297.5	-3.25	300.25	208	2.4	19.0	2756

The symbols below will be indicated alongside shares and can be interpreted as follows:

'A' alongside a share name indicates that it carries no voting rights.

♣ indicates that investors can get a free copy of the company's latest reports and accounts.

♥ this indicates that the stock is not listed in the UK.

♠ this indicates an unregulated collective investment scheme.

Xd means that the recently declared dividend will still be paid to the previous owner of the share.

Xr indicates the same for a rights issue- i.e. the buyer will not be acquiring the right to subscribe to the new issue of shares.

Xc means that the buyer does not get a scrip issue of shares which the company is issuing in lieu of a dividend.

Interpreting the figures

Interpreting the figures is largely self- explanatory.

1. The first column – notes - lists the company name.
2. The second column – price – shows the average (or mid price) of the best buying and selling prices quoted by market makers at the close of market on the previous day, the close being 4.30pm. If trading in the share has been suspended for some reason then this is denoted by a symbol and the price quoted is the price at suspension. The letters 'xfd' following a price mean ex-dividend and indicate that a dividend has been announced but this will not be available to new purchasers.

3. Price change. This will be plus or minus depending on the movement of the shares. This column will give the change in closing price compared with the end of the previous day.

4. Previous price movements. The fourth and fifth columns show the highest and lowest prices recorded for the stock during the past 12 months.

5. Dividend yield. The sixth column shows the percentage return on the share. It is calculated by dividing the dividend by the current share price.

6. Price earning ratio (P/E). The seventh column is the market price of the share divided by the companies earnings (profits) per share in the last 12 month trading period. Yields and P/E ratios move in opposite directions: if the share price rises, since the dividend remains the same, the dividend yield falls; at the same time, since the earnings per share are constant, the P/E ratio rises.

7. The last column, 8, deals with the number of shares traded the previous day rounded to the nearest 1,000.

How to use the information effectively

The first indicator to look at is that of price. The price is the current price of a share. This needs to be looked at in conjunction with the 52 week high and low in order to get some kind of historical perspective of performance of the company.

The prices quoted are the mid-prices between the bid or buying price and the offer or selling price at which market makers will trade. The difference between bid and offer is known as the spread and it represents market makers profit on any given transaction. The implication of the spread is that investors will only be able to buy at a higher price and sell at a lower price than that quoted in the newspaper.

Volume is an indication of the liquidity of a stock, or how easy it is to buy and sell. High volume is much more preferable than low volume but take into account the fact that smaller companies are traded much less heavily than larger companies. Volumes will also be higher when a company makes an announcement.

The dividend yield is a reflection of the way that the market values a company. If the company is thought to have a high growth rate and is deemed to be a secure business, then its current dividend yield will be low, since the scope for increasing dividends in the future is average.

The dividend, to some degree, is an arbitrary figure, decided at the whim of a company. The figure for the yield is not always a good indicator of the vale of a share. Price/earnings ratios are generally better as they are independent of arbitrary corporate decisions.

Price/earnings ratios are the most commonly used tool of stock market analysis. Essentially, they compare a company's share price with its annual earnings, indicating the number of years that it would take for the company, at its current earning power, to earn an amount equal to its market value. Shares are often described as selling at a number times earnings or on a multiple. In general terms, the higher a company's ratio the more highly rated it is by the market. High price/earnings ratios are usually associated with low yields. A high ratio suggests a growth stock and is, like a low yield, an indicator of an investment where capital growth might be more important than income.

Evaluation of weekly performance

Monday's edition of the financial times will indicate weekly changes in share prices. The column will look as follows:

Weekly tables

1	2	3	4	5	6
7	8				

Notes	Price	WK% Change	Div	Div Cov	Mcap £m	Last XD	City line
BAE Systems	♣288.25	4.3	9.5	1.8	9,262	20.4	1890
Chenning	476.5	1.3	9.4	3.9	138.6	11.5	2116

The weekly column indicates:

1. Notes-the name of the company
2. Price with relevant symbol
3. The weeks price change as a percentage
4. Dividend – the dividends paid in the last financial year
5. Dividend cover - the ratio of profits to dividends, calculated by dividing the earnings per share by the dividend per share. This indicates how many times a company's dividend to ordinary shareholders could be paid out of net profits
6. Market capitalisation – this is an indication of the stock market valuation of the company in millions of pounds. It is calculated, as we saw earlier, by multiplying the numbers of shares by their market price.

7. Ex-dividend date – this is the last date on which a share went ex-dividend, expressed as a day and month unless a dividend has not been paid for some time. On and after this date, the rights to the last announced dividend remain with the seller of the stock. The share register is frozen on the xd date and the dividend will be paid to the people on the register at that time. Until it is paid, buyers of the share will not receive the next payment due.

8. Cityline – the FT Cityline code by which real-time shares are available over the telephone by calling 0906 003 or 0906 843 plus the four-digit code for any given share. This telephone information service is designed primarily for investors wanting to keep track of their own investments or the activity of the UK and world stock markets at any point.

The key information from this listing is that of dividend cover. This indicates how safe the dividend is from future cuts. The higher the figure the better able a company will be to maintain its dividends if profits fall.

Other share dealings

Financial times share price coverage is expanded on a weekly basis on ft.com to cover dealings in securities that are not included in the standard share information service. Information is provided on name and stock type plus price.

Trading volume

The back page of the companies and markets section has a useful reference table with the trading volume and basic price information for the constituents of the FTSE Index, the index of the top 100 UK companies. This will deal with the largest capitalised and most actively traded stocks, discussed further on.

Trading volume, price and change in stocks are indicated in this table. Trading volume is an indication of the liquidity of a stock. The higher the figure, the easier it will be to buy or sell significant quantities of stock without having a major impact on its price.

The FT carries three other lists for quick reference on share price movements.

Share rises and falls

This table, shown daily, shows how many securities rose, fell and stayed at the same price level during the previous trading session. It is broken down into nine different categories of security and shows how movements in the main share price indices were reflected in trading across the various market divisions.

Highs and lows

This table shows which shares have, on the previous day reached new high or low points for the past 12 months. The highs and lows table highlights company's that are moving against the general trends of their sector.

Main movers

This table will indicate the stocks that had the biggest percentage rise and falls the previous day. It will indicate the name of the company, the closing price, the days change as a price and percentage.

Winners and losers

Saturday's FT includes a table of the FTSE winners and losers. This lists the top and bottom six performing companies over the previous week in three sectors (the FTSE 100, the FTSE 250 and the FTSE SmallCap sector). Included will be their latest price, percentage price change on the week and change on the start of the year. It also lists the six top and bottom performing industry sectors.

There are price tables for unit trusts and gilts. Gilts are normally split into short, medium and long-dated. There are also two undated ones and index-linked stocks. Foreign governments also issue bonds that are listed.

Indices

Newspapers also print information for the movement of specific industrial sectors, plus some describing the type of share. These are then aggregated to form wider industrial indices such as Basic Industries, General Industrials, 650, All Share and so on. The Financial Times produces a full list of the FTSE indices compiled and calculated under formulae developed by actuaries.

Every stock market has its indices to show movements in the market as a whole. Different papers report different selections of these. As mentioned previously, some of the better known ones are the Dow Jones, Nasdaq, Standard and Poor's, Toronto 300. Nikkei, Hang Seng, Dax for Germany, CAC40 for France and the Toronto Composite Index. There is also a table for the highest volumes of trade.

Papers such as the Financial Times will also provide invaluable editorials and views of experts which should be studied carefully as they are quite often right and can steer investors away from potential problems.

10. Choosing a Share

Choosing a share

This can be one of the easiest or hardest activities. As we have seen, shares in the largest companies generally tend to be stable and it is not too hard to forecast movements. Picking a share in one of these companies is therefore relatively unproblematic. However, problems come when a more adventurous approach is needed.

Fundamental analysis

One approach to choosing shares is that of fundamental analysis. This looks at the business and products of a company and also looks at its accounts, examining earnings and prospective dividends. Other factors such as the economy are examined along with the rate of inflation, level of currency, consumer demand and interest rates. In addition, economic competitors are examined along with efficiency of management. The analyst will then decide whether the business is adequately or fairly valued by the market.

Fundamental analysis concentrates on the true value of the company and then checks whether the share price reflects the true value. Nearly all the calculations are done by published accounts. Accounts reveal a wealth of information other than basic economic information and can demonstrate whether or not a company is doing well and stable or whether it is heading for trouble.

For the private investor, the process of identifying companies that are undervalued and therefore worth investing in is daunting, given the amount of companies in the UK. Also, given the amount of stockbrokers in the UK most of the companies have been covered anyway.

For the private investor there are ways of spotting potential companies to invest in. The answer is to have a set of personal criteria within which you will act. You can stick to companies with a P/E ratio of no more than five or six, or with a yield at least 10% above the average. You can look at neglected sectors and try to analyse what the future trends are likely to be. Combine all the information to hand with other information such as consumer confidence, the state of the economy etc and this can provide the basis of a fundamental rational analysis.

Technical analysis

In contrast to fundamental analysis we have technical analysis, also known as Chartism. This is concerned with the movement of share prices in the recent past to try to gauge how they will do in the future.

Technical analysis ignores the underlying worth of the business. It is not concerned with efficient management but only when the market price is likely to change. The main point is to identify patterns and to deduce whether there is likely to be any significant movements.

Ethical investments

In addition to the numerous ways of choosing a share to buy, ethical considerations come into play with some investors. There are several arguments put forward in favour of ethical investments. The most common one is that it is the correct way to invest. If investment is carried out blindly, you could be in the situation where on one hand you might deplore a war or invasion but find out that you are in fact investing in a company that is manufacturing arms and selling them to the warring parties. Similarly, you might deplore the state of the environment but find out that you are investing in a company that is doing its share of raping the land.

Obviously, choosing a company is a matter of personal choice and so is the fact of drawing the line. Many companies have been shunned over recent years. In the bad old days of apartheid in South Africa, Barclays Bank was held up as a culprit as it conducted big business there. Tobacco companies have been shunned, oil, paper, timber (deforestation) mining, pharmaceuticals and so on. Companies have also been boycotted because of their negative polices on pollution, ozone depletion and waste management.

For the individual investor it is better to have a specific set of criteria within which to work as confusion can set in and probably rule out a vast number of companies, whose end business is making money. There are specific unit trusts that have been created to cater for ethical investors and many fund managers can point you towards one. It is fair to say that not many have had a lot of success.

Sources of information for the small investor
Market signals

A sure sign that something might be up is when a company buys back its own shares. This is usually an admission of failure to manage. It shows that there are no more remunerative sources for the corporate cash in investing in the business. Either this, or the business is trying to boost its earnings per share figure without changing the fundamentals.

Director's dealings

Companies are obliged by law to inform the market about dealings in their shares by directors of the company. This will go out on the stock exchange news system. Directors may provide very plausible reasons for selling shares, but if this is the case then it is better to be cautious and find out what the situation is. Why did the director sell shares in his own company? It could be that money was needed but it is still better to find out.

Using stockbrokers to advise on shares

This might seem the obvious answer, to utilise experience. However, any investor needs to be up to date with the markets in order to understand the advice given to him by stockbrokers. This is because the advice given may not always be the best advice. Again, it is imperative to do your own analysis, both technical and fundamental, as outlined in this book, and not to jump in straightaway when a decision has been taken to buy shares. Look at all the factors, very subjective economic factors and also past and present performance before committing yourself. Read the newspapers, look at the figures and scrutinise the editorials so that you at least have a semblance of knowledge and can have a reasoned conversation with the professionals.

11. Interpreting company accounts

Company accounts

We discussed company accounts in a previous chapter, how a potential investor can glean information about a company's health from looking at key indicators in accounts.

It is tempting just to read financial pages and make a decision about the health of a company from information contained therein. However, if you want to make a serious attempt at investing in shares then the first thing you should do is to obtain a copy of the company accounts, or the annual report, either from the company itself or from companies house.

There are a number of key indicators from which you can measure a company's performance. They are all contained within the annual report. There are several crucial indicators, which in addition to being in the accounts are published in papers such as the financial times each day. These are dividend yield and the price earnings ratio and also dividend cover.

For the small private investor the most useable of the key indicators are the return on capital employed, gearing, income gearing and pre-tax profit margin. Using the three mentioned above together with these four the private investor will be able to judge whether or not the company is a sound investment.

Key financial ratios

The four financial ratios, return on capital employed, gearing, income gearing and pre-tax profit margin are reasonably easy to work out. In annual reports they will be over a two-year period so that changes over time are reflected. Often, a report will include a section on 'facts for shareholders' or a five year record which include some calculated ratios. However, quite often these ratios are calculated in certain ways and it is always better to carry out your own calculation. Below is an indication of the basic calculation of the key ratios.

Gearing

Gearing compares the amount of money in shareholders funds with the amount of external liabilities that the company has. High gearing is more risky than low gearing as it means that a higher level of external liability exists. This, of course could be for many reasons, such as company expansion and so on.

There are a number of ways of calculating gearing but one of the main ways also effectively highlights a company's exposure and vulnerability. The ratio is a comparison between the total debt liabilities of a company and its shareholders funds. The more the debt and the higher the interest payments the lower the profits and the lower potential for paying out dividends of any worth.

To make the calculation: find current liabilities in the annual report, often called 'liabilities: amounts falling due within one year'. Add 'creditors: amounts falling due after more than one year' ensuring that everything is included, to find total debt liabilities. Next, find the figure for total shareholders funds, but do not include minority interests. Divide total debt liabilities by total shareholders funds and multiply by 100 to arrive at a percentage figure.

The rule of thumb is as follows:

Low gearing = below 100%

Medium gearing = 100-200%

High gearing = above 200%

Income gearing

This ratio demonstrates a company's ability to service its debt. Income gearing will reveal this information. It is the ratio of interest payable to the profits out of which that interest must be paid. Obviously, all companies wish to keep interest payments as low as possible.

Philip Green, the owner of BHS and other stores, famously ensures that debt is paid off as soon as possible in order to maximise the overall profitability of his companies.

A lot of investors regard income gearing as the most important ratio. To calculate income gearing: find the interest payable for the year, which is often expressed as a detail in the notes. The figure on the balance sheet is 'net interest' which is interest payable minus interest receivable. Find the earnings, or profit, before interest and tax. Often this must be calculated by adding interest payable to the pre-tax profit shown on the profit and loss account. Divide interest payable by profit before interest and tax and multiply by 100 to express it as a percentage.

The outcome can be read as follows:

Low income gearing = below 25%

Medium income gearing = 26-75%

High income gearing = above 75%

Return on capital employed

This measure is an indicator of how efficiently management is performing. It relates pre-tax profit to the level of long-term capital invested in the business. It is a good guide as to whether enough return is being generated to maintain and grow dividends and avoid future cash flow problems.

To calculate ROCE: capital employed is equivalent to total assets minus current liabilities and this figure is usually demonstrated on the balance sheet. If it isn't then it should be calculated as long-term debt, plus provisions for liabilities and charges, plus any other long term liabilities, plus shareholders funds, plus minority interests. Divide pre-tax profit by capital employed and multiply it by 100 to express it as a percentage. The calculation should be interpreted as follows:

Low profitability = below 10%

Medium profitability = 10-20%

High profitability = above 20%

Pre-tax profit margin

This ratio will reveal the profits earned per pound of sales and therefore measures the efficiency of the operation. It is an indicator of the company's ability to withstand adverse trading conditions such as falling prices, rising costs or declining sales.

To calculate the pre-tax profit margin: take the pre-tax profit figure on the profit and loss account. Divide it by the total sales revenues (sales turnover) and multiply it for a percentage. The calculation can be interpreted as such:

Low margin = below 2%

Medium margin = 2-8%

High margin = above 8%

The above is a basic guide which will enable you to read and interpret a company's accounts and to gain a clearer idea whether or not to invest or steer clear.

12. Taxation

Shares and taxation

The area of tax and share dealing has always been a bone of contention.

Dividends

Dividends on shares are usually paid net of tax and the voucher that comes with the payment notification will contain details of a tax credit. People who do not normally pay income tax cannot reclaim the tax already paid on the dividend, and people paying tax at the basic rate need pay no further tax on the income.

People who pay tax at the higher rate have to pay at 32.5% of the gross, though the credit detailed on the slip is set off against this. Essentially, about a quarter of the net dividend is due in tax for higher rate payers.

Scrip issues of shares in lieu of dividend are treated in a similar way. There is no tax to standard rate payers and the higher rates are assumed to have had a 10% tax credit.

If the company buys back shares then the tax situation is the same as a dividend.

Capital profits

A profit on the sale of shares is liable to tax for profits above the basic tax-free allowance. Capital gains tax is only a problem for those people who deal in large amounts of stocks. Windfall shares received from demutualized building societies or insurance companies are counted as having cost nothing and anything made from their sale is counted as a capital gain, unless they have been put into a tax sheltering scheme such as an ISA.

There is a tapered tax relief however, so holding a share for a long time will reduce the tax liability. If the shares were bought before April 1998 the price rise can be adjusted for inflation before tax is payable. Dealing costs in buying and selling are allowable against the total gain and there is also an allowance for part paid shares. Gifts between spouses are tax free, so a portfolio can be adjusted to obtain the maximum allowance.

Losses made from selling shares in the same tax year can be set off against the profit. If any of the companies go bankrupt, the shares are seen to have been sold off at that date for nothing and the capital loss from the purchase can also be set off against any gains made.

Share schemes

Receiving shares from an employer counts as pay and is subject to income tax. If the employee buys the shares at a discount to the market price, the employee will pay tax on the discount.

Under approved profit-sharing schemes the company can allocate tax-free shares to workers, although there are many rules attached to this.

Enterprise investment schemes

Investment in newly issued shares of an unlisted company can be set off against income tax at a reduced rate, but the full relief both in income and capital gains taxes comes only if the shares are held for years. Losses can be set off against either capital gains or income. Capital gains can also be deferred by rolling the investment over: after selling the proceeds from one investment it can be invested in another and no tax paid until the investment is realised.

Venture capital trusts

This is a version of Enterprise Investment Schemes. Tax breaks are almost the same but the investment is in a quoted financial vehicle, which will invest the cash in a variety of businesses. The risk is therefore reduced by spreading over a number of ventures.

The above is very brief and for more in depth advice you should refer to an accountant experienced in these matters.

Glossary of terms

Alternative Investment Market – the area of the stock market for small companies or those too young to meet the requirements for full listing

Authorized share capital – the amount of shares that a company may issue

Bear market – a time of falling share prices

Bid – the price at which managers of unit trusts will buy back the units from investors, compared with the offer at which they sell units

Blue chip – a highly rated company and its shares

Bond – a tradable fixed interest security

Bonus issue – this is another name for scrip issue or the distribution of shares to existing shareholders at no cost to them

Bull market – a time of rising share prices

Common stock – American term for ordinary shares

Convertible – a class of paper issued by companies (such as loan stock or preference shares) that can be converted into ordinary shares at a preset price, on a set date

Coupon – the interest rate on a corporate bond

Crest – the stock exchanges electronic register of share ownership to replace paper certificates

Dividend – this is an amount of money paid out to the holders of shares, based on an amount per share

Easdaq – European Association of Security Dealers Automated Quotation System

Equities – ordinary shares

Ex-dividend – a share that is sold soon after a dividend being announced with the seller still getting the payment

Flotation – bringing a company to the stock market to get its shares publicly traded

FTSE 100 – the top 100 companies in the UK with the highest market capitalisation

Fundamental analysis – looking at the company behind the share. This is in contrast to technical analysis which looks only at movement in share prices

Gearing – a ratio of a company's borrowings to its equity

Gilts – short for gilt edged, the name used for government bonds

Hedging – protecting against a potential liability

Insider – someone with access to privileged information. It is illegal to trade shares when in possession of such knowledge

Issued share capital – these are the shares that a company has actually sold

Leverage – the American term for gearing

Liffe – London International Financial Futures and Options Exchange

Liquidation – the sale of an insolvent company's assets to pay creditors

Liquidity – a measure of how easy it is to trade shares. Also used to assess assets by how readily they can be turned into cash

London Stock Exchange – the largest stock exchange operating in Britain

Members – the shareholders of a company

Nasdaq – National Association of Securities Dealers Automated Quotation System. This is a New York based system with an emphasis on companies using advanced technology

Net asset value – all the assets of a company minus all its liabilities and capital charges

Ofex – a computerised stock market run by market maker P Jenkins, founded in 1995

Offer – the price at which managers of unit trusts sell the units to the public

Price/ earnings ratio - this compares the current price of the share with the attributable earnings per share

Put option – the right to sell a share at a set price within the period of the agreement

Registrar – the organization that maintains the record of a company's shares and their ownership

Rights issue – a way of raising money by selling more shares sometimes giving people who own shares the right of first refusal in proportion to the shares that they own

Seaq – this stands for stock exchange automated quotations and is the electronic system that displays the bid and offer prices for securities by market makers, together with the size of the parcel that they will deal in

Share premium – if the nominal value of a company's share is 30p but it issues them at 50p the 20p difference is in the books as the share premium account

Shareholders funds – the assets of a company minus its liabilities; since shareholders own the business what is left belongs to them

Spread – the difference between the buying and selling price of a share or other asset

Stockbroker – a professional dealer in shares who acts as an agent for the investor

Technical analysis – another name for a chartist way of looking at the market

Warrants – a type of investment allowing the holder to buy paper from the issuer at a fixed price sometime in the future

Yield – this is calculated by taking the amount of a dividend as a percentage of the current share price. If a share stands at 100p a dividend of 10p represents a yield of 10%.

Useful addresses

Association of Investment Trust Companies 24 Chiswell Street London EC1Y 4YY 020 7282 5555 www.aitc.co.uk

Association of Private Client Investment Managers and Stockbrokers 114 Middlesex Street London E1 7HY 020 7247 7080 www.apcims.co.uk

Association of Unit Trusts and Investment Funds 65 Kingsway London WC2B 6TD 020 7831 0898 www.investmentfunds.org.uk

Banking Ombudsman 70 Gray's Inn Road London WC1X 8NB 0345 660902.

Chart Analysis 020 7439 4961

Chartered Institute of Taxation 12 Upper Belgrave Street London SW1X 8BB 020 7235 9381. www.tax.org.uk

Companies House
www.companieshouse.gov.uk

Ethical Investments Research Service 80-84 Bondway Bondway London SW8 1SF. www.eiris.org

Financial Services Authority 25 The North Colonnade London E14 5HS 020 7676 1000 www.fsa.gov.uk

Investments Ombudsman 6 Fredericks Place London EC2R 8BT 020 7796 3065

Investors Compensation Scheme Financial Services Compensation Scheme, 7th Floor, Lloyds Chambers, Portsoken Street London E1 8BN 020 7892 7300.

London Stock Exchange, 10 Paternoster Square, London EC4M 7LS 020 7797 1000.

London International Financial Futures and options Exchange Cannon Bridge London EC4R 3XX 020 7623 0444 www.liffe.com

Nasdaq www.nasdaq.com
New York Stock Exchange
www.nyse.com

Securities and Futures Authority (SFA) 25 The North Colonnade, Canary Wharf, London E14 5HS. 020 7676 1000.